Why Am I Afraid to Love?

by John Powell

Argus Communications

Designed by
Patricia Ellen Ricci

Published by
ARGUS COMMUNICATIONS CO.
7440 Natchez Avenue
Niles, Illinois 60648

International Standard Book Number: 0-913592-03-x

WHY AM I AFRAID TO LOVE?

TABLE OF CONTENTS

Beloved,
let us love one another,
because love takes its origin in God,
and everyone that loves
is a child of God
and knows God.
He who has no love
does not know God,
because God is love.
God's love
was made manifest
among us
by the fact that God
sent his only-begotten Son
into the world
that we might have life
through him.
This love consists
not in our having loved God
but in his having loved us
and his having sent his Son
as a propitiation
for our sins.
Beloved,
if God so loved us,
we in turn
ought to love one another.

1 John 4: 7-11

1 MAN'S INVITATION TO LOVE

The word *religion* is derived from a Latin word *religare,* which means *to bind back.* By his practice of religion man binds himself back to God who is his alpha (origin) and omega (destiny). To anyone who is familiar with the New Testament there can be no doubt that the essential act of religion and the essential bond between man and his God is *love.* When Jesus was asked by the Pharisees: "Which is the greatest commandment?" he answered:

> *"You must love the Lord your God with all your heart, with all your soul, and with all your mind. This is the greatest and the first commandment. The second resembles it: You must love your neighbor as yourself."*   Matthew 23: 35-39

What does it mean to love God with one's whole heart, soul and mind? I think that St. John would answer this question by telling us that before anyone can really give his heart, soul and mind to God, he must first know how much God has loved him, how God has thought about him from all eternity, and desired to share his life, joy, and love with him.

9

Christian love is a response to God's infinite love, and there can be no response until one has somehow perceived that God has first loved him, so much so that he sent his only-begotten Son to be our salvation.

More than this, God does not simply *have* love; he *is* love. If *giving* and *sharing* with another is the character and essence of love, then God is love. He can acquire nothing because he is God. He needs nothing because he is God. He has all goodness and all riches within himself. But goodness is self-diffusive; it seeks to share itself. So the infinite goodness which is God seeks to communicate, to diffuse, to share itself . . . with you . . . with me . . . with all of us.

We know something of this love in our own instincts to share that which is good and is our possession: good insights, good news, good rumors. Perhaps the best analogy in our human experience is that of the young married couple, very much in love and very much alive because of that love, wishing to share their love and life with new life which it is in their power to beget. But it is even more than this with God who tells man: if the mother should forget the child of her womb I will never forget you!

It is precisely this that is the point of most failures to love God truly. Most of us are not deeply aware of his fatherly, even tender, love. It is especially the person who has never experienced a human love, with all of its life-giving effects, who has never been introduced to the God who is love through the sacrament of human love, that stands at a serious disadvantage. The God of love who wishes to share his life and joy will probably seem like the product of an over-heated imagination — unreal.

There is no human being who will not eventually respond to love if only he can realize that he is loved. On the other hand, if the life and world of a person is marked by the absence of love, the reality of God's love will hardly evoke the response of his whole heart, soul and mind.

False Gods Before Us

The God who enters such a life will be a fearsome and frowning idol, demanding only fear of his devotees. The *Book of Genesis* tells us that God has made us to his image and likeness, but it is the most perduring temptation of man to invert this, to make God to his human image and likeness.

Each of us has his own unique and very limited concept of God, and it is very often marked and distorted by human experience. Negative emotions, like fear, tend to wear out. The distorted image of a vengeful God will eventually nauseate and be rejected. Fear is a fragile bond of union, a brittle basis of religion.

It may well be that this is why God's second commandment is that we love one another. Unselfish human love is the sacramental introduction to the God of love. Man must go through the door of human giving to find the God who gives himself.

Those who do not reject such a distorted image will limp along in the shadow of a frown, but they certainly will not love with their whole heart, soul and mind. Such a God is not loveable. There will never be any trust and repose in the loving arms of a Father; there will never be any mystique of belonging to God. The person who serves out of fear, without the realization of love, will try to bargain with God. He will do little things for God, make little offerings, say little prayers, etc. to embezzle a place in the heaven of his God. Life and religion will be a chess-game, hardly an affair of love.

Response to God's Love

The person who is open to the realization of God's love will want to make some response of his own love. How can he make a meaningful response if this God cannot acquire and needs nothing? St. John points out the place of human response:

We know what love is from the fact that Jesus Christ laid down his life for us. We, too, ought to lay down our lives for our brothers . . . Beloved, let us love one another, because love takes its origin in God, and everyone that loves is a child of God and knows God. He who has no love does not know God, because God is love . . . No one has ever seen God, yet if we love one another, God abides in us and our love for him reaches perfection.

1 John 3:16; 4:7-12

Meeting God in other humans is the most costly part of the dialogue between God and man. The nature of man requires that he somehow contact God in a bodily or sensibly perceptible way. In the Old Testament God came to man in thunder and lightning over Sinai; his voice emerged from a burning bush. In the New Testament God's goodness to man is even more astonishing: He becomes a man and is raised in agony on a cross for you and me. "This is what I mean when I say I love you." In the Incarnation God brought his gifts to man in the earthen vessel of humanity that He might speak our language and we might know what he is really like.

Just as God expected men to find him under the veil of humanity, even when that humanity was a red mask of blood and agony, so now he expects men to find him under other human veils. It will, indeed, cost a man a great deal if he takes God seriously on this point:

". . . For I was hungry, and you gave me to eat; I was thirsty and you gave me to drink; I was a stranger and you took me into your home; I was naked, and you covered me; I was

sick, and you visited me; I was in prison, and you came to see me."

Then those who are saved will say to Him: "Lord, when did we see you hungry and feed you? or thirsty and give you to drink? And when did we see you a stranger and take you into our homes? or naked and cover you? When did we see you sick or in prison, and come to visit you?"

And in explanation the King will say to them: "I tell you the plain truth, whatever you did to the least of my brethren, you did to me!"

Matthew 25: 35-40

The early Christians did not distinguish love of God from love of man; in fact they had one word, *agape*, to describe the one love that simultaneously embraces the God of love and the least of his brethren.

But all this is old stuff, isn't it? Sometimes when we grow stale, there is a temptation to think that it is really God's Word that is stale. When the dimensions of generous response seem shrunken in us, we are tempted to turn away from the real issue, to look for more practical, relevant issues to discuss.

This is a dangerous thing to do: to avoid confrontation with the real challenge of God's Word. Someday we shall all inevitably meet him. The danger of embarrassment is great. He just might ask as he extends his hands to greet us just beyond the door of death:

"Where are your wounds?"

It just might be that, with St. Augustine, who wrestled a long time before succumbing to grace, we shall have to say:

"Too late, O Lord, too late have I loved you."

The Meaning of Love

Whatever else can and should be said of love, it is quite evident that true love demands self-forgetfulness. If there are many people who use the word and claim the reality without knowing the meaning of the word or being able to love to any great extent, this is the test: *Can we really forget ourselves?* There are many counterfeit products on the market which are called love, but which in fact are falsely named. We can sometimes label the gratification of our needs "love"; we can even do things for others without really loving. The acid test is always the probing question of self-forgetfulness.

17

The person that
Each of us is —
is unique.

Can we really locate the focus of our minds on the happiness and fulfillment of others? Can we really ask not what others will do for us, but only what we can do for them? If we really want to love, then we must ask ourselves these questions.

We must become aware that we are capable of using people for our own advantage, for the satisfaction of our deep and throbbing human needs, and be deluded into thinking that this is really love. The young man who professes to love a young woman may often be deceived in thinking that the gratification of his own egotistical urges really constitutes love. The young woman who finds the voids of her own loneliness filled by the companionship and attention of a young man may well mistake this emotional satisfaction for love. Likewise, the mother and father who anxiously try to promote the success of their children can easily rationalize their desire for the vicarious experiences of success and convince themselves that they are loving parents. The critical question always remains that of self-forgetfulness. Does the young man or woman, the mother or father really forget himself and his own convenience and emotional satisfaction, to seek only the happiness and fulfillment of the beloved? These are not merely theoretical questions. The fact of the matter is that, for most of us, our own needs are so palpable and real to us, that it is enormously difficult for the seed to fall into the ground and die to itself before it can live a life of love.

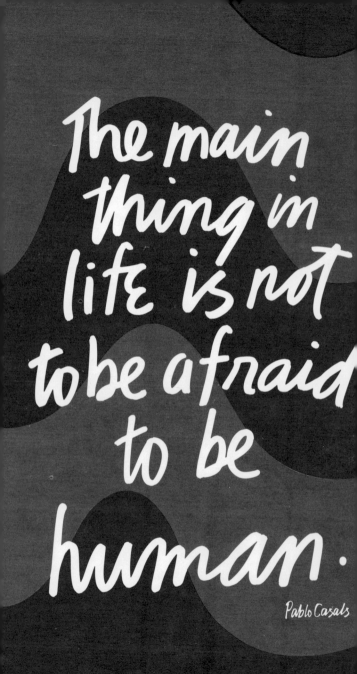

The main thing in life is not to be afraid to be human.

Pablo Casals

2 HUMAN PAINS IN A LOVELESS WORLD

All of us to some extent are enduring agonies of loneliness, frustration, emotional and spiritual starvation. Somehow these pains are radically due to failures in love. The essential sadness of such pain is that it magnetizes the focus of our attention; it preoccupies us with ourselves. And self-preoccupation is an absolute obstacle to a life of love.

I once asked a Psychiatrist friend of mine, "How can you teach people to love?" His answer was mildly surprising, to say the least. He answered the question by asking one of his own: "Did you ever have a toothache? Of whom were you thinking during the distress of your toothache?" His point was clear. When we are in pain, even if it be only the passing discomforts of an aching tooth, we are thinking about ourselves.

The Psychiatrist continued: "This is a pain-filled world in which we are living. And the pains that reside deep in the human hearts around us are not like toothaches. We go to bed with them at night and we wake up with them in the morning. Two-thirds of all the hospital beds in this country are now occupied by mental patients. One out of ten Americans has already been treated for mental illness. The pain inside of them simply became too deep and required professional attention. The suicide rates in the eighteen to twenty-one year age group is extremely high. Suicide ranks as the third highest killer in this age group. In the twenty-one to twenty-four year age group, it is the fourth highest killer. This is a pain-filled world, and so, a loveless world that we live in. Most human beings are so turned-in by their own pains that they cannot get enough out of themselves to love to any great extent."

Person and Personality

Each of us is a unique and individual *person*. We sometimes facetiously remark to others: "After God made you, he broke the mold." In fact, each of us is fashioned in a unique mold. There never has been and never will be anyone exactly like you or me. However, at the beginning of life this person is, as it were, like the bud of a flower or plant: closed. Only when the bud of the flower receives warmth from the sun and nourishment from the mothering soil will it open and expose all of the beauty that is latent within it. So, too, the human person at the beginning of life must receive the warmth of human love, assurance and the nourishment of parental affection if it is to open and expose the unique beauty that God has placed within every human individual.

Personality, in the sense which we are adopting here, is the social manifestation or expression of *person.* We express ourselves and the unique personal beauty radiated in us in various ways. This process of opening and self-revelation is what psychologists call the *dynamics* of human personality.

We know that if the bud of a flower is injured by hostile forces, like an unseasonal frost, it will not open. So, too, a human person who is without the warm encouragement of love, and who must endure the chilling absence of praise and affection, will remain closed in on him-

25

The book of Genesis says that God created man to His image and likeness. It seems that the most enduring heresy in all of Christian history has been this —

that man has reversed genesis –
man has made god to his
image and likeness.

self. The dynamics of his personality will be jammed. And, if the dynamics of personality are seriously impeded, the result will be what psychologists call *neurosis*. Although there are many valid descriptions of neurosis, neuroses are commonly recognized in the form of a crippling inability to relate well to others, to go out to them and to accept them as they are without fear of rejection.

The First Seven Years of Life

Those who have been driven by their discomfort to seek professional help from a clinical psychologist or psychiatrist are often surprised that the doctor evinces particular interest in the earliest memories of his patient's childhood. It is the unanimous consensus of psychologists that our basic personalities are fairly well formed in the first seven years of life. Although it is a truth which most of us find ourselves reluctant to accept, it is quite obvious that we do retain the psychological traits which we manifested at age seven for the rest of our lives. If we were quiet and predominately inward at that age, the chances are that we are still quiet and inward; if we were boisterous extroverts at age seven, the chances are that others still have to bear with our boisterous extroversion.

Although it is difficult to accept, the psychological scars that we have acquired during these first seven years remain in some way with us for life. No very deep psychological problems originate after this age, although these scars and scar-tissue may be aggravated or inflamed by circumstances occurring later in our lives. The rather common prejudice is that we are personally the masters of our fates and the captains of our souls; the truth of the matter is that we are very largely shaped by others, who, in an almost frightening way, hold our destiny in their hands. We are, each of us, the product of those who have loved us . . . or refused to love us.

Anxiety

There are three basic emotional problems with which all of us must, to some extent, live. The first of these is called *anxiety*. Anxiety may be described as *the irrational fear of an unknown object*. We are not quite sure what it is that is bothering us, but we are aware of the uneasiness in our minds and the effects of this uneasiness in our nervous system and digestive tracts. To the extent that we bear the scar-tissue of anxiety, we fear that something is wrong or will go wrong. The deeply anxious person lives his life under *Murphy's Law:* "What can go wrong will go wrong." Murphy's Law is illustrated each time that we drop our toast. It always lands jam-side down.

The defense mechanisms built into human nature are many and complicated. Nature seems to seek its own anesthetics. For example, when we are enduring such great physical pain that the threshold (endurance capacity) of pain is crossed, nature often seeks the anesthetic of unconsciousness. We faint. Insanity itself is a common refuge for those who find life unbearable. It is an escape from a real and too-painful world with which the individual finds it impossible to cope.

So with anxiety, human nature has its own built-in defense. Nature tends to constrict the general fear of anxiety into particular fears called *phobias.* A phobia can be defined as *an irrational fear of a known but unrealistic object.* Rather than submit to the constant uneasiness of anxiety, nature seeks to relieve us by constricting and restricting this general fear into particular moments. There are many people, for example, who look under their beds at night before retiring, even though they have found nothing but dust there for many years. There are others who cannot endure the cloister of a closed-in place (claustrophobia). Others are unable to endure the possible perils of a high place (acrophobia). These phobias, designed to spare us from the constant tremors of anxiety, are usually many and deep-seated in the seriously anxious person.

Causes in the genesis of anxiety are not easy to trace. Psychologists, however, are becoming increasingly aware of the importance of what are called *pre-natal experiences.* When a woman is carrying a child, the child is on its mother's bloodstream. Hematology (the study of blood and its diseases) has revealed the changes in blood chemistry which occur during the traumatic moments of human life. We are all aware of the physical effects of our emotions, of the adrenalin flushing into our blood streams, the palpitating heart and the beads of perspiration that form on our foreheads and in the palms of our hands.

The fetus or embryo, forming in its mother and nourished by her bloodstream, experiences these same impulses and effects. They are also transmitted by the muscular contractions of the mother's body, which the fetus likewise experiences. The fetus records these experiences and retains them both in its braincells and nervous system which is formed during the period of gestation. When a woman is consistently upset emotionally during this period of pregnancy, the child to be born will receive and retain the message, transmitted via blood chemistry and muscular contraction: this is a very insecure world into which it is coming.

We also know that the infant after birth is very sensitive to the hands that hold it. If it is dropped quickly or moved quickly, this abrupt and unexpected motion causes an immediate nervous reaction. The infant will arch its back and its muscles will stiffen. Only gradually will those muscles relax and become supple again. Infants do not hear soft sounds, but sudden loud noises shock the infantile nervous system; again the back will arch and stiffen, the muscles will become tense and rigid. Consequently, the nervous hands and abrupt movements, the exploding voices of the infant's parents will tend to reinforce the message of anxiety, which will be retained in the brain cells and nervous system of the child for life.

Very often we call the seriously anxious person a "worry-wart." We tell these persons, in our naivete and lack of compassion, that they shouldn't worry. We even accuse them of looking for things to worry about. Actually the person who is given to worry has very little control over these instincts, and our lack of compassion is hardly of help to him.

The Guilt Complex

The second basic emotional affliction, to which all of us are to some extent heirs, is called *the guilt complex.* The first thing that must be said about this guilt complex is that it is unrelated to actual

There is such a thing as a peace
of soul approach to religion. It
makes of God a gigantic Bayer
aspirin ... take God three
times a day
and you won't feel any pain.

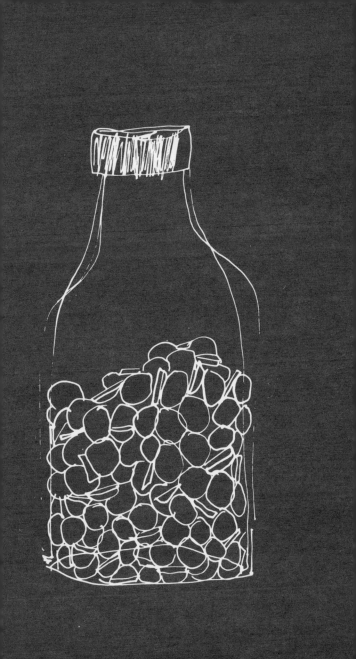

guilt. In fact, its origin is usually traceable to an age when serious, actual guilt would be impossible. A guilt complex may be described as *a haunting sense of moral evil or sinfulness*. The person who vividly experiences a guilt complex is constantly haunted by his own deep feeling of sinfulness or evil. This complex also carries with it *a need to be punished.* Although it sounds rather bizarre, the person who is deeply afflicted by a sense of guilt, will seek his own punishment unknowingly and unconsciously.

In its extreme manifestation the deeply "guilty" person will tend to hurt himself physically or to confess some crime of which he is not guilty. In a lesser but more common manifestation, the person may well seek a partner in marriage or the companionship of another who he thinks will punish him. It is not uncommon for a woman who has been married to, and suffered from, an alcoholic partner in marriage to remarry, after the demise of her first husband, another alcoholic. In fact there is a counterpart of Alcoholics Anonymous called Alinon for the wives of reformed alcoholics. The emotional adjustments of living without punishment can, in some cases, be very great. This is not to say that all of the members of Alinon are the bearers of deep guilt-complexes, but simply that this could be one of the emotional adjustments that must be made in the wake of alcoholic reform.

As with anxiety, human nature has its own devices to lessen the suffering of the guilt complex. Just as anxiety tends to constrict itself into the phobia, so the guilt-complex tends to constrict itself into what are called *scruples*. The word scruple is derived from the Latin word, *scrupulum*. A *scrupulum* is a small pebble. When by accident a small pebble gets lodged inside one of our shoes, as we walk along we feel the intermittent stabs of pain. So the scrupulous person, as he walks through life, feels the intermittent agonies of his imagined guilt. A scruple usually centers around some supposed sin or guilt. Just as the phobia constricts and concretizes the generalized fear of anxiety, so does the scruple constrict and concretize the generalized sense of guilt. Consequently, the bouts with scruples, precisely because they are intermittent, spare the deeply-guilty per-

Love is
Essentially
a
relationship

son from the generalized and constant agony of his complex.

The origin of the guilt complex is usually traceable to severe or harsh parents. Perhaps such parents have explained to themselves that their severity is designed to produce well-disciplined children. They justify their outbursts of emotional rage and the ventilation of their own personal discomfort under the holy name of "child training". When these outbursts become a pattern of parental conduct, the children of such parents may well bear the scars of their "training" for the rest of their lives in the form of guilt complexes.

Not long ago a woman named Ruth Krause wrote a book called *A Hole is to Dig.* In this book she relates the answers of groups of children asked to define many of the common realities of life. "Arms," one child wrote, "are to hug." "Puppies are to jump all over you and lick your face." "A hole is to dig." The deeper intent of Miss Krause was to illustrate that children do not think as adults. When, for example, a parent leans down over his small child, with blood in his eyes and flames snorting from his nostrils, and in a terrifying voice shouts: "You *bad* boy! You crossed the street, and I told you not to!" the child will have little reason to understand the dangers of crossing a street. He does not know, because he does not think in terms of cause and effect, the perils of a small child crossing the street alone. He will, however, retain this message: he is *bad.* Margaret Mead, in her book, *And Keep Your Powder Dry,* insists on the necessity of conveying to a child a sense of being loved even when he is being scolded or punished. Punishment in anger is almost always, if not always, a very dangerous thing.

The Inferiority Complex

The third basic emotional affliction of man is called the *inferiority-complex.* It is *a sense of inadequacy as a person.* The person who feels deeply inferior, as we all do to some extent, may be aware of certain particular abilities, but there is inside of him the gnawing parasite of his own inadequacy. He feels that he is unacceptable as a person. He feels that he has very little personal worth. As opposed to the victim of a guilt-complex, the person afflicted with an inferiority-complex will feel not so much a sense of moral evil but of worthlessness. The genesis of the inferiority complex is, like the other emotional scars that we bear, traceable to one's very early life. When parents treat a child as though he were their bag and baggage, and train him to a constant state of surrender to the almighty parental will, they are sowing the seeds of such a complex.

Dr. Benjamin Spock feels that the rigid enforcement of eating times and habits, and the rigid regulation of the other biological functions of a child's body, can well upset the emotional balance of that child for the rest of his life. The message transmitted by mothers who do not wish to reheat food and fathers who will not tolerate a floor full of toys at any time, because it is inconvenient to them is: "You have no worth of your own. Your whole good is to go along with us, and not to rock the boat of our convenience." This is not to issue an indictment against a reasonable and loving discipline of children. Obviously, children must learn that others have rights, and a child must be trained to realize that he is to respect the convenience of others. However, when this training is exaggerated, the child is led to believe that his whole worth is to respect the desires and convenience of his parents. He will, then, instinctively conclude that he has no worth of himself, a lesson that will sabotage his self-confidence, perhaps for life.

It should be noted that most of the effective lessons that a child needs in order to be prepared for life are taught rather by example than by angry or severe words. When we wish to teach a child how to blow up a balloon, we do not give a set of verbal instructions, and expect the child to absorb them. A child is not so much a thinker as an imitator. So we blow up the balloon ourselves, allow the air to escape, and ask him to do the same thing. Being such an instinctive imitator, he can do it almost at once. The parents who disguise the love of their own convenience under the title "child training" are teaching their child habits of self-centeredness which can bring only unhappiness. We have said that the first seven years of life are the critical years, and much of what is called the *basic human option,* either to *love* (to seek others and their happiness) or to *lust* (to seek self and one's own gratification), will be determined by the lessons of parental example and the osmosis of childlike imitation.

3 THE SELF IMAGE

It is almost a truism in contemporary psychology that one's image of himself lies at the root of most human conduct. What is more difficult to accept is that the image each of us has of himself is really the product of what other people, rightly or wrongly, have told us that we are. If one imagines himself to be evil or inadequate and his life to be governed by Murphy's Law, it will show in his conduct. He will attempt nothing of challenge and will consider safety as that which must be sought above and before all. He will somehow attempt to hide his shame or inadequacy under a veil of anonymity. The one thing he cannot do— and it is the one thing every human being must do to be fully alive—is accept himself as he is.

The whole theory of Dr. Carl Rogers, famous for his non-directive or client-centered system of counseling, is based on the need for self-acceptance. Dr. Rogers maintains that the basic challenge of every human life is that of self-under-

YOU BETTER NOT
COMPROMISE
YOURSELF.
IT'S ALL YOU GOT.

JANIS JOPLIN

standing and self-acceptance. He further postulates that no one can understand and accept himself as he is until another has first understood and accepted him for what he is. Finally, Rogers maintains that, once we have been accepted as we are and loved for what we are, the symptomatic problems with which most of us struggle in life will yield to this self knowledge and acceptance.

Consequently, Rogers suggests that the role of a counselor (and this might well be applied to the role of a friend) is largely to listen as the client describes his problems and ultimately himself. He must convey a sense of acceptance to his counselee, without yielding to the impulse of saddling him with gems of advice and direction. To be successful at this type of counseling or friendship, one must make an act of faith that the great human need is to know and accept oneself as he is. We are too often tempted to think that putting another in his place, or taking him down a peg, or forcing him to face reality is the pathway to solution. In fact, harsh criticism that hits at the person rather than the deed only deepens the problem because it makes self-acceptance more difficult.

Recently a plastic surgeon discovered that when his surgical arts had removed some physical ugliness or assisted a person to a more pleasing physical appearance the patient frequently underwent a transformation of personality. He became more confident, more outgoing, and exhibited a newly emancipated human spirit. In pursuing his investigation of this phenomenon, he turned to the inner image, as opposed to the external physical appearance, and discovered that this inner self-image controls so much of human conduct and happiness. In his book, *Psycho-Cybernetics,* Dr. Maltz depicts the ugly self-image as the radical cause of most human inertia, failure and unhappiness.

The importance of one's self-image is aptly illustrated in the fairy tale *Rapunzel.* It is the story of a young girl, imprisoned in a tower with an old witch. The young girl is in fact very beautiful, but the old witch insistently tells her that she is ugly. It is, of course, a strategem of the witch to keep the girl in the tower with herself. The moment of Rapunzel's liberation occurs one day when she is gazing from the window of the tower. At the base of the tower stands her Prince Charming. She throws her hair, long and beautiful golden tresses, out the window (the root-ends, of course, remain attached to her head), and he braids the hair into a ladder and climbs up to rescue her. Rapunzel's imprisonment is really not that of the tower but the fear of her own ugliness which the witch has described so often and so effectively. However, when Rapunzel sees in the mirroring eyes of her lover that she is beautiful, she is freed from the real tyranny of her own imagined ugliness.

This is true not only in the case of Rapunzel but with all of us. We desperately need to see in the mirror of another's eyes our own goodness and beauty, if we are to be truly free. Until this moment, we, too, will remain locked inside the prison towers of ourselves. And, if the thrust of love requires us to be outside of ourselves and to be preoccupied with the happiness and fulfillment of others, we will not love very much until we have had this vision.

When you repress or suppress those things which you don't want to live with you don't really solve the problem because you don't bury the problem dead — you bury it alive.
It remains alive and active inside of you.

Ego Defense Mechanisms

We have already mentioned that human nature is resourceful in the matter of self-defense. This resourcefulness is perhaps nowhere better illustrated than in the ego defense mechanisms which we employ to protect ourselves from the chimeras of anxiety, guilt, and inferiority complexes. Rather than expose a self which we imagine to be inadequate or ugly, we instinctively build walls, contrary to Robert Frost's advice: Do not build a wall until you know what you are walling in and what you are walling out. To the extent that we experience scars of anxiety, guilt, and inferiority feelings, we are tempted to wear masks, to act roles. We do not trust or accept ourselves enough to be ourselves. These walls and masks are measures of self-defense, and we will live behind our walls and wear our masks as long as they are needed.

While it may seem to be a safer life behind these facades, it is also a lonely life. We cease to be authentic, and as persons we starve to death. The deepest sadness of the mask is, however, that we have cut ourselves off from all genuine and authentic contact with the real world and with other human beings who hold our potential maturity and fulfillment in their hands. When we resort to acting out roles or wearing masks there is no possibility of human and personal growth. We are simply not being ourselves, and we cannot emerge in an atmosphere of growth. We are merely performing on a stage. When the curtain drops after our performance we will remain the same immature person that we were when the curtain went up at the beginning of the act.

Very often our masks are obviously pretentious or ugly. The small boy walking through the dark cemetery in the dead of night whistles to convince himself and others who may be with him that he is not afraid. We call it "whistling in the dark". We know that the small boy, who dreams of becoming a basketball star, walks on the tips of his toes, trying to be something that he fears he isn't. More obnoxious perhaps is the person who bites his nails inwardly but wears the pretentious mask of cockiness on the outside. Eventually the public which sits in attendance on such an act sees through it.

There is a strong human temptation to judge people only in terms of these acts or masks. It is all too rare that we are able to see through the sham and pretense of masks the insecure or wounded heart that is being camouflaged and protected from further injury. Consequently, we lash out with the iron fists of criticism and sarcasm or we try to tear off the masks of our fellow men in ferocious anger. We fail to realize that masks are worn only as long as they are needed. Only the reassurance of an accepting and understanding love will lure the anxious, the guilt-ridden and the supposedly inferior persons out from behind their defenses. It may well be that we ourselves are hiding behind such masks and walls, resulting in very little human encounter and communication . . . only mask facing mask, wall facing wall.

Generally, we can recognize masks. We have a sense that our brother is not authentic, that he is pretentious, and we call him a sham. We very much dislike

most men lead ves of quiet desperation.

—Thoreau

the mask of belligerence, and we resent the silent mask of the sphinx. We try to sabotage the complacent mask of cockiness in the young and the mask of arrogance in the old. We do not realize that in the unexposed roots of these exteriors, there is only a cry of pain and the need to be understood and loved into life. Most of the obnoxious qualities that we find in others are the result of some kind of defensive convergence on self, and we openly resent this self-centered posture. It is then that we must remember the psychiatrist's question: "Did you ever have a toothache?" We must learn to look through the sham and pretense of our fellow human beings, to alleviate the pain and the lonely voids that have constructed these defense walls. Direct attacks on these defenses will only produce their reinforcement.

The Subconscious Mind

Psychologists tell us of two levels of the human mind: the *conscious* and the *subconscious.* It is obvious from the terminology itself that we are conscious or aware of the contents of our conscious minds; we are unaware of the contents of the subconscious levels of our minds. These two levels of the mind have been compared to the upstairs and downstairs of a human dwelling. When we find eyesores, a worn-out piece of furniture or an unsightly pail of garbage, we instinctively want to put them out of our sight —into the basement, where we will not have to look at them. So it is with the two levels of the mind. When we cannot face or live with some reality or attitude that we find in ourselves, we can submerge this reality or attitude into our subconscious minds. When we wish to forget some *event* of our lives, and deliberately hide it in the confines of the subconscious, this is called *suppression*. When we discover some *attitude* or *emotional reaction* in ourselves, which we consider unworthy and therefore put out of sight and into the subconscious mind, this is called *repression*.

Eventually, when the subconscious mind becomes overloaded, we find ourselves very uncomfortable. We are unaware of the exact source of our discomfort, precisely because our real conflict has been buried in the subconscious. What we bury there is not buried dead but alive, and remains alive. Sometimes we try to find an antagonism of the present moment upon which to lay the blame for our discomforts, but the roots of our pain can be found only in the subconscious mind.

For example, when a child is not loved and not given a sense of his own personal worth by his parents, he will tend to react in one of two ways: he will take the path of external conformity or external rebellion. But there will always be a resentment because he has been deprived of his psychological needs. However, society and our culture will not allow us to express this resentment, real as it may be. When the child tries to express this resentment to his parents, they will remind him forcibly that they are his parents and deserve to be loved. The fact of the matter is that they may not be loveable and their insistent demand to be loved will place the child in a position of deep emotional conflict. Parents who are adamant in their insistence that their children obey the fourth commandment to honor father and mother should make an equal effort to be honorable.

The child, in whom inevitable resentment is growing, usually cannot express this resentment and is made to feel that it is a very evil thing. Should he try to express this to others outside of his family, he may well be called an ingrate and made to feel ashamed for having such an attitude towards his parents.

The stage has now been set for repression. Not knowing what to do with his resentment he will hide it in the basement of his mind. It is like a splinter of wood that has been pushed deeply under the flesh where it will fester and cause agony; the resentment in the child who is not loved will be a source of much pain. There is always the chance that this resentment, gathering too much force in the subconscious mind, may boil over into acts of violence or vandalism, and the wrong people may have to bear the brunt of this hidden or repressed resentment.

Another example of a common repression is the repressed need for affection and love. Very often in our culture such needs cannot be acknowledged or expressed. They do not coincide with the image of independent virility that is thrust upon us by our society and culture. Consequently, the person who has these repressed needs will have to seek their gratification in devious and subtle ways, at times deceiving even himself.

It has been said that liquor, in releasing inhibitions, often opens the door to the repressions in the subconscious. The person who becomes argumentative and antagonistic under the mild influence of liquor is probably releasing his repressed hostilities. The person who wants to put his arms around everyone in the place, male or female, may be releasing something of his repressed needs to be loved. We will recall that in T. S. Eliot's play, *The Cocktail Party,* the author portrays a man under the influence of liquor leaning over to a psychiatrist at the Cocktail Party. He pleads with the psychiatrist for this favor: Please make me feel important.

And this is what *psychoanalysis* is all about. The analyst dredges the contents of the subconscious mind, helps the person to realize what his problems really are, and tries to help him to live with them.

Although hypnosis and narcotherapy (the use of truth serums) are sometimes used in psychoanalysis, the most common means is called *free association*. The person is helped by the analyst to associate his present thoughts with memories of his past, and gradually, to link what he feels in the here and now to the historical and radical causes of these feelings. He may also attempt to interpret his client's dreams, the matter for which is supplied largely by the subconscious mind since the conscious mind is not active during sleep.

Needless to say, the process of psychoanalysis should be left to those who are professionally competent. The only point in bringing this up is to illustrate the reality of the subconscious mind and the fact that we very rarely understand our own motivation and the root causes of our own discomfort.

Transference

Very often we are strongly impelled by the needs that exist at subconscious levels. The need to be loved, to feel important, and the need for self-acceptance

can very often, even when we are unaware of it, have a profound influence on our conduct and dealings with others. *Transference,* in the sense that we are here using it (it does have another usage), is always *a subconscious process by which we transfer our needs to others.* For example, if we wish to feel important, we may seek to lord it over others, to dominate them. If we were to be asked about such conduct we would heartily and intransigently maintain that this is the way that others need to be treated. It is for their own good. Actually, we may be transferring our own subconscious need to them. A young person may well enter upon an occupation of notable altruism on the grounds that he wishes to make a contribution to a needy world. While this may in fact be the case, it may also be that subconsciously he has an unsatisfied need to be needed.

Very often when mothers or fathers are over-protective of their children, on the alleged grounds that they wish no harm to come to them, they may well be subconsciously transferring their own need to have their children dependent upon them. They do not want them to grow up. While it is well for us to be aware of this possibility of transference in our lives, to be aware that we may well be seeking ourselves under the guise of altruism and love, there is really no way to lay open all the intricacies of human motivation or to explore our own subconscious needs. The only effective measures that we can take are to renew our motivation and to locate the focus of the mind on those we are trying to serve and help. If we can consistently do this, we will gradually acquire the habit that is called love.

The Need For Professional Help

Our age has been called "the age of the couch". Sometimes we interpret the presence of stress and strain in our lives and inside of ourselves as an indication of the need for professional psychological or psychiatric help. The stigma of seeking such professional help has largely been removed in these times, perhaps due to the admission of many movie stars and national heroes that they have sought and been helped by such professional treatment. However, suppression, repression, subconscious needs and transference are a part of the psychological makeup of all of us. Hopefully, not all of us stand in need of such professional help.

We have mentioned at the beginning of this book the dynamics of human personality and the possibility that these dynamics can become impeded. If they are impeded to such an extent that the person is able to neither experience true, meaningful human friendship nor perform in reasonable proportion to his capacities, there is then indication that he is in need of professional help.

A true and meaningful human friendship supposes more than mere association with another. It supposes that we are able to share ourselves, to reveal ourselves to another who is our friend. It supposes that we can entrust him with our secrets and accept his confidences. It is the human relationship that Martin Buber calls the "I-Thou" encounter.

There is always some gap between our absolute potential and actual performance. None of us ever fully realizes his absolute potential nor translates perfectly his best intentions into external accomplishments. Yet, when there is a considerable gap between potential and performance, as when the student of considerable intellectual endowment cannot pass his courses in school or when the competent worker cannot perform sufficiently to hold a job for a very long time, there is some indication that the dynamics of personality have been seriously jammed and there is need of professional assistance.

A further indication of this need may arise from what are called *psychosomatic illnesses.* Because of the mysterious interrelation of soul and body, the buried disturbances of the mind may express themselves in physical reactions. Again, this should be left to the professional judgment of a competent physician. And finally, prolonged *depression* which indicates the presence of some disturbance within the person can be an indication that the person is in need of professional help. There are times, of course, when we all feel depressed. The depression that is symptomatic of a deeper problem is usually a crippling and prolonged depression. But again it will be expressed in the inability of the person involved to

67

accomplish a meaningful friendship and to perform in reasonable proportion to his ability.

The Need For Friendship

While the person in need of professional help should seek out competent and professional assistance, all of us have the need for the supportive psychotherapy of friendship. We are, each of us, a conglomeration of mysterious needs and impulses which need to be ventilated. We need to be able to express ourselves, to talk ourselves out without fear of rejection by others. Too often the problems that we keep submerged within us remain, in the darkness of our own interior, undefined and therefore destructive. We do not see the true dimensions of these things that trouble us until we define them and set lines of demarcation in conversation with a friend. Inside of us they remain as nebulous as smoke, but when we confide ourselves to another we acquire some sense of dimension and growth in self-identity and the capacity to accept ourselves as we are.

It may well be that our walls and masks will make this difficult. We may instinctively try to rationalize that there is really no one near to whom we can talk ourselves out. Many of us practice the self-deception of believing that there is no one in our supposed circle of friends that can be trusted. Very commonly these excuses that we have rehearsed so often are merely excuses. Our real fear is that we would be rejected, that the other person would not understand us. And so we wait and wait and wait behind our walls for the sufficient sound of reassurance in another or we gaze out of the windows of our towers looking for a Prince Charming to come and rescue us. We excuse ourselves from all initiative in seeking a truly human, interpersonal relationship with another on the grounds that the time is not ripe or the circumstances right. In the meanwhile, we can only perish. We will very likely "act out" the problems that remain submerged within us if we refuse to "talk out" these problems. We will act out our hostilities by destructively criticizing those around us, or act out our need to be loved by an emotional overdependence upon others.

Our lives are
shaped by those
who love us —
by those who
refuse to love us.

We will act out our repressed sense of inferiority by trying to humiliate others or dominate them.

It is so much wiser to take all the risks of confiding in another than to live alone behind walls and masks, blindly acting out the things that we refuse to talk out. And we must remember, if we want to love others truly, that these repressed and suppressed problems are very definitely impediments to love. They are our toothaches which keep us converged on ourselves, keep us from being ourselves, and keep us from forgetting ourselves.

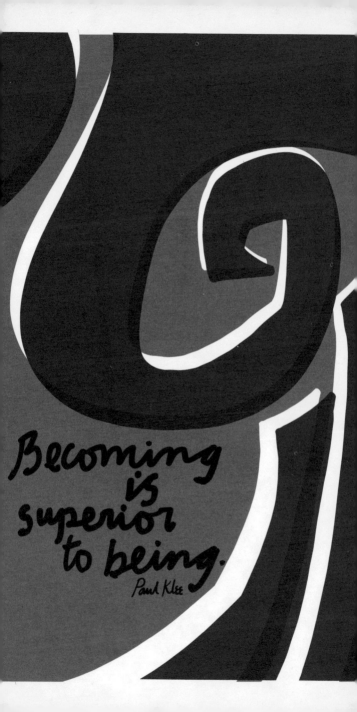

Becoming
is
superior
to being.

Paul Klee

4 THE MATURING PROCESS

We speak of people as being mature or immature, but the fact is that all of human life should represent an ever-continuing growth towards full maturity. What we have called the dynamics of human personality are very much involved in this process of self-revelation and of self-expansion. Consequently, all the signs of immaturity are somehow characterized by convergence upon self. This self-centeredness betrays itself in many ways: bearing grudges and prejudices, pouting, emotionalized thinking, exaggerated feelings of inferiority, over-concern about the opinions that others have of us, worrying, overdependence upon parents or family, rebellious and angry attitudes, bragging or bullying, temper tantrums, the negativism of destructive criticism, procrastination, self-indulgence, "slapstick" humor which is humiliating to another, flirtations, etc.

The patterns of maturity are recognized in the ability to go out to others, to get along with them, to exercise a reasonable self-sufficiency, to set realistic goals, to exercise discretion, to differentiate the important and unimportant things in life, flexibility, adaptability, and emotional stability.

We might divide human maturity into four different aspects. *Intellectual maturity* is characterized by the ability to form one's own opinion, respecting but not leaning on the opinions of others; the ability to make one's own decisions, with all due respect to substantial evidence and the counsel of others, independently and firmly. The intellectually mature person is willing to change his mind in the light of new and important evidence and to modify his plans if such seems to be wise. He has his own thoughts, makes his own decisions and accepts full responsibility for them. He is willing to bear responsibility and to acknowledge the truth even when it is displeasing, or makes serious demands of him. He does not approach his problems by worrying over them. He analyzes the problem, considers the alternatives, makes a decision, executes and lives with that decision.

Emotional maturity is characterized by the acceptance of emotions together with the ability to keep them under reasonable control. The emotionally mature person can live with emotional situations without falling apart, and he learns to deal with these situations objectively. He talks out grievances rather than pouts; he can accept criticism without feeling deeply hurt; he can face and do unpleasant things without running away from them; he is not overcome by childish fears and anxieties. Both the radical, who wants to change everything from the ground up, and the reactionary, who does not want anyone to rock the boat and who is deeply devoted to the *status quo,* are emotionally immature, as Martin Peck points out in his book, *The Meaning of Psychoanalysis.*

Both the radical and the reactionary represent an unresolved attitude toward domineering parental authority, long after the reality-situation has ceased to exist. The radical has sought to rebel and has never outgrown this rebellious attitude. The reactionary has chosen to conform and for his own reasons will tend to be a conformist all of his life. He will fear to attempt new accomplishments on

Never build a wall
until you know what
you're walling
in — and what you're
walling out.

his own and he will be reluctant to accept whatever is new.

Social maturity is characterized by the ability to go out to others, to relate well with them, and to accomplish meaningful friendships. The socially mature person is neither too dependent on his own family or friends, nor does he wage war with them. He can adjust himself to the laws and conventions of the society in which he lives; and he is able to subordinate himself to the prosecution of group ideals and group needs. He finds that work can be interesting, in spite of its unpleasant and humdrum aspects.

Moral maturity is characterized by the devotion to moral ideals and the ability to live them out. A child's morals are generally instinctual and unreasoned. They are the morals of his parents and those around him. In adolescence, the morally maturing person will conceive his own ideals and will have a method of arriving at them which is fairly definite and intelligent. With ever-deepening maturity, a person's ideals usually become more realistic and consistent, and at the same time firmer. In general it can be said that the morally mature person has come to his ideals in a perspective that is altruistic rather than egocentric.

Since maturity is an ever-evolving process and progress, it can be marked by halts *(fixations)* and recessions *(regressions)*. There are in each of us two conflicting tendencies; to grow up and to turn back. In general when life demands more of us than we feel capable of giving, we develop what has been called "promotional neurosis". We have difficulty in adjusting to increased responsibilities to tend to back away.

H. Crichton Miller in his book *The New Psychology And The Teacher* suggests that the two most common causes of fixation and/or regression are 1) *domineering parental authority,* and 2) *a too harsh presentation of reality.* Domineering parental authority stifles individuality and self-expression; a person can mature only to the extent that he is allowed to be himself. He is a unique person and must be allowed to be and express what he is. A presentation of reality which seems too harsh is puzzling to a child and becomes too much for his powers of

81

adjustment; and so he does not follow his predominantly biological urge to grow up, but fixates or regresses to escape the challenge.

Fixation represents an arrested emotional development. It is usually a case of apron strings, "smother love," and excessive dependence on the thoughts and decisions of others. *Regression* is a returning to a lower stage of development; it is living in the past. "Backward, turn backward, O Time,/In your flight./Make me a child again, just/For tonight." (Elizabeth Akers Allen) It is the "Old Oaken Bucket Complex" (cf. poem by William Wordsworth): "How dear to this heart are the/Scenes of my chidlhood,/When fond recollection presents them to view." Memory often distorts the possibilities of the past, and glamorizes what might have been. (cf. Wendell White *The Psychology Of Dealing With People*, p. 75.) Regression is well-illustrated in the so-called "grown-up" who delights in the college reunion or business convention so he can act like a "kid" again.

Regression is usually a return to a point of previous fixation. For example, the devoted daughter, who was the little darling of her parents, may be impelled to run home to them when her marriage becomes difficult. She may want to regress to the stage or point of fixation when she was a little darling; she refuses to accept the challenge of being a grown-up mother and wife. The dominant motive for such regression, as we have said, is usually the reluctance to accept new challenges and responsibilities.

Children who have been pampered (and this applies chiefly to the ages of three to twelve), who have been given everything and asked nothing, are often pre-disposed to regress later in life to cantankerous and childish bids for attentions. Frustrations and anger, also, if carried inside of a person too long without the ventilation of conversation with another, tend to result in regression.

Maturation and Needs

Infancy is the period covering the first two years of life. We must recall what we have said about anxiety and its transmission during infancy. Here the stress must be placed on the positive needs of the child at this stage. The infant's chief need is for tender love which is communicated primarily through the sense of touch. If an infant is shown much love and given the sense that he is loveable during this period, he will grow up to expect friendliness from others and be more disposed to love others himself. It should be remarked that infancy is a human being's first impression of life. In general, it is necessary that this first impression be one of security, tenderness, and love. Infancy is not the stage in which children can be "spoiled".

Childhood embraces the third to the twelfth year of life. It is during this period that a person begins to establish his own individuality and self-esteem. Parents must guard against the two extremes of over-protection and rejection. Children who are over-protected, for whom parents do everything and whose every activity is supervised with eager parental eyes, are never taught the self-reliance that is a part of growing up. They are not being prepared to accept hardships. They are not being trained to make responsible decisions.

The greatest accomplishment during the period of childhood is training in socialization. A child must be taught to share and cooperate, to relinquish the self-centered world of the infant. About the age of three a child tries to grow into relationships with others; and at the same time he is busy trying to become a unique somebody. When he becomes frustrated or disoriented by this double effort, he comes into what is known as "the age of resistance". He resorts to hostile refusals. He may try to return to being a baby again, or introvertedly to turn away from reality. He may try to console himself with thumb sucking; he might exhibit spiteful rebellion, resist feeding, and stage temper tantrums. However, by age five he usually recovers and has developed a clearer concept of his own personal status and the wisdom of adult authority.

The most critical problem in childhood is that of *discipline*. The central directive is this: give as few commands as are strictly required and then see that they are carried out. To give too many commands will seem justifiably unreasonable to a child and he will rebel. During this period, parental discipline should gradually yield to self-discipline. Only by practice can a child develop self-reliance and a sense of personal responsibility.

A second very serious problem which often occurs in this stage is that of *jealousy*. If the older child isn't given some time exclusively for himself and some explanation that the new baby has more needs, is more helpless, etc., his jealousy can lead to anger and even hatred of his parents. There might also occur in him feelings of failure and shame and possibly a lasting resentment for the younger child who is the object of his jealousy. Usually this jealousy can be forestalled by giving the older child rights of seniority, by encouraging him to help with the care of the baby, and by consistently reminding him of his own unique personal worth.

Adolescence is the period that extends by definition from age twelve to twenty-one. Adolescence has been called the period of "storms and stress". Our American type civilization creates much of this strain, storm and stress by its own

... I feel the capacity to care
is the thing which gives life
its deepest significance.
Pablo Casals

pressures and choices. For example, the young person must decide about going to college, accepting political affiliation, achieving self-support, choosing a profession, and establishing wholesome relationships with the opposite sex.

In our American culture parents often unknowingly employ certain means that deepen the storm and stress of adolescence. This is depriving the young of emotional security by offering or withdrawing signs of affection as a source of coercion. So many parents offer signs of love only on the condition of surrender to their will and whims. Likewise, many parents goad their children into a relentless pursuit of success by threatening to withdraw their love in case of failure. This threat of rejection subjects children to serious emotional strain by making them feel that they must be good or smart, etc. In general, children can endure serious emotional strain from other sources if the tender and loving care of their parents is present.

The main conflict in the adolescent is between two tendencies: *gregariousness* and *individuation.* The adolescent seeks to be accepted by others (gregariousness) and at the same time he seeks to be himself (individuation). Conformity appears to be the price of popularity, and yet it asks the submission of individuality. Adolescents who make this submission slavishly do not build up a sense of who and what they really are, and are consequently confused. Conformity to the peer group and the acceptance of the many status symbols of adolescent society can tend to imprison young men or women just when they are seeking to be free and to be themselves. The more acceptance an adolescent receives in his own home and from his own family, the less he will be subjected to the pressures of his peer group and the less he will be inclined to conform to their arbitrary standards.

The tension is concretely between social acceptance and the denial of individuality. The adolescent is torn between the achievement of personal confidence and underlying uncertainty. He sincerely questions answers given him, yet he can appear very sure of himself. This sureness is usually a compensatory cover or mask for his uncertainty. The doubts he

The REAL

that God is
DEAD

ARE supposed to
WHO STAND AS

AND Especially

HE IS
DEAD IN US —

NEVER

PROBLEM IS not

ut THAT WE WHO
EFLECT GOD AND
ymbols of God
or THE young

ECAUSE WE HAVE
UNDERSTOOD
HIM.

has are encouraging symptoms of intellectual awakening. He questions authority and even his religious faith. He is trying to make his convictions his own. He must never be scolded for this. It is the time of life when he most needs the sensitive sympathy of his parents.

The adolescent is especially sensitive to criticism and disparagement. He needs abundant affection, encouragement, praise and attention to counteract the demoralizing experiences of the classroom, the athletic field and the scramble for social acceptance. Bragging or belittling others is only his way to conceal personal insecurity, and its importance should not be exaggerated. Those who volunteer to "take him down a peg" do him a great disservice.

The most serious adjustment of the adolescent is the emancipation from family bonds. Overprotective or possessive parents are terribly frustrating to him, and he may develop an allergy for all authority as a result. He may even try to appear to be dirty or disheveled to serve notice to the world that all parental training in cleanliness has been successfully rejected. The emancipation that should be taking place during this time involves ". . . emergence from parental supervision, reliance upon the security that one can give himself rather than upon the security provided by parents, development of an attitude toward parents as friends rather than as protectors and supervisors, planning of one's own time and making one's own decision without over-bearing parental control." (cf. Luella Cole, *The Psychology of Adolescent,* 3rd edition, p. 7.)

The problem of the sexual urge is a very real source of confusion to the adolescent. If he is to learn the true relationship between sex and love, it is important that he feel free to discuss these matters openly and without shame with his parents. He must be helped to accept his new sexual feelings as normal, natural and good. He must also learn the wisdom of self-control. Sexual indulgence is very commonly a sign of regression to primitive and infantile forms of satisfaction and gratification. To mature in this matter of sexuality will generally bring with it total maturation; to fail to grow in this area usually causes fixations or regression. Sexual indulgence does not afford a much needed feeling of security nor will it satisfy affectional and emotional needs. If, however, the affectional and emotional needs of adolescence are satisfied in controlled relationships with members of the opposite sex and within his own family, the sexual urge will be far easier for the adolescent to control. Masturbation and other efforts at sexual self-gratification are usually symptomatic of retardation or regression in personal development. Such indulgence educates the deepest neuro-vegetative instincts in man to seek primarily personal gratification. Unless these instincts are correctly educated in adolescence, there will be a deep and permanent stamp of selfishness on the person at the instinctual level, and this will be a serious, if not insuperable, obstacle to the ability to love.

Positive vs Negative
Reinforcements of the Will

Sometimes we speak of the will as though it were a muscle, either strong or weak. This manner of speaking can easily obscure a very important reality about human conduct. The will is not itself weak or strong in us; it is rather our *motivation* that is weak or strong. It is also important to realize that *reasons* for good conduct are not the same as *motives*. We might well enumerate many good reasons for doing this or that, but they are not motives unless they move us. The Latin word *movere* means "to move" and it is this word from which our word motive is derived.

Because, as we said in the beginning, every person is unique, it is also true that what will move one person might well leave another cold. If a good reason is to become a motive for the will, its goodness must be somehow exposed to the person in question. The imposition of authority cannot, in itself, produce virtue; it may well produce conformity, but conformity is not always virtue. Virtue must come from within a person. It must be the product of an interior act of the will seeking a good, and the will responds only to motives whose good is recognized.

Psychologists, in studying human motivation, have found that *positive* reinforcements of the will (reward for good conduct) are infinitely more effective than *negative* reinforcements (punishments for bad conduct). To be constantly critical of a young person is obviously a dangerous thing. It tends to undermine his confidence and to make all authority obnoxious. However, if one takes the approach of positive reinforcements, tending to overlook small failures in conduct but never failing to recognize and reward (at least with a kind word) the desired conduct, the effect will be almost magical. It is an illustration of the power released in the creation of a good self-image: most people will be in their conduct what we tell them they are.

If we build pedestals, young people will climb up on them; if we keep our hands on the edge of the rug, always ready to pull it out from under them, there can only be trouble ahead.

CAUTION

HANDLE
WITH CARE

unless you
love someone
nothing else
makes any
sense. ee cummings

5 LEARNING TO LOVE

The whole process of maturation depends on *how we react* to the difficulties or challenges of life. The immature person sees only the difficulties: they are so close to his near-sighted eyes that he can see only the problems and pays very little attention to his own reaction which is, in fact, the critical and definitive thing. Difficulties pass, but our reaction to them does not. As William James has suggested, there may be a God in heaven who forgives us our sins, but human nature does not. They are memorized in our minds, muscles, fibers, and brain-cells. Each reaction, mature or immature, lingers on in us as the beginning of a habit. Repeated mature reactions tend to produce the formed habits of maturity which define us. Repeated immature reactions dig their own grooves.

The Christian must always accept himself in his present, pilgrim and human condition, which will inevitably involve failure. Ideals must always be introduced to the test of actual experience, and in this introduction our ideals, which very often sound beautiful, become a struggle, a renunciation, a battle for control of self, a willingness to start again in the wake of failures, a lucid acceptance of the mystery of the cross.

It is not the problem, and in this case not the isolated *failure* that is critical, definitive, and paramount. It is our *reaction to it*. The reaction of the Christian must always be suffused with a confidence nourished by the conviction that God and he are a majority, even stronger than his own weakness. The process of maturation as a Christian and as a human being will inevitably be marked by failures, but the only real failure is to quit. When the situation gets tough, the Christian must get tougher. He must become bigger than his problems. In the end, such determination to love will bring him to the feet of Love itself, which is his eternal victory in the victorious Christ.

The Paradox of Love

All of us experience at some time or another a feeling of loneliness and isolation, a very painful void inside of ourselves that becomes an unbearable prison. We have all felt at some time alienated from others, separated from the group, alone and lonely. By its very nature this loneliness, like all of our toothaches, centers the focus of attention on ourselves. We seek to fill this void, to satisfy this hunger . . . we go out to find others who will love us.

We may do things for them in an obvious attempt to gain their love. We may come to them with hands stretched out like pan-scales. On the one hand is our donation to them, the other hand being extended to receive their donation to us. We may even be deceived into thinking that this is loving.

We know that our loneliness can be filled only by the love of others. We know that we must feel loved. The paradox is this: if we seek to fill the void of our own loneliness in seeking love from others, we will inevitably find no consolation but only a deeper desolation. It is true that "You're Nobody Till Somebody Loves You." Only the person who has experienced love is capable of growing. It is a frightening but true reality of hu-

God does not create in order to acquire something but in order to give something ... only to share Himself.

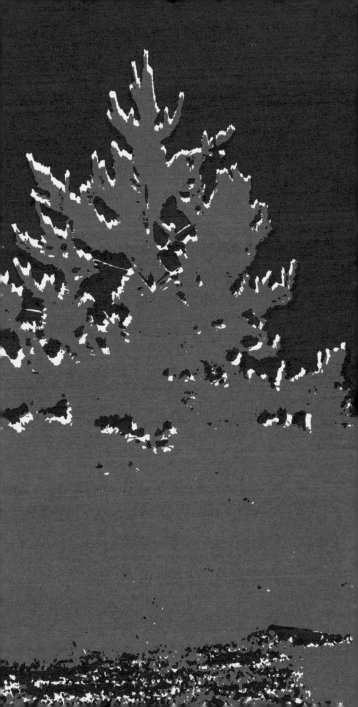

man life that, by loving me or refusing to love me, others hold the potential of my maturity in their hands. Most of us, driven by our own aching needs and voids, address life and other people in the stance of seekers. We become what C. S. Lewis, in his book, *The Four Loves,* calls ". . . those pathetic people who simply want friends and can never make any. The very condition of having friends is that we should want something else besides friends." Most of us know our need to be loved and try to seek the love that we need from others. But the paradox remains uncompromised; if we *seek* the love which we need, we will *never find it.* We are lost.

Love can effect the solution of our problems, but we must face the fact that to be loved, we must become loveable. When a person orients his life towards the satisfaction of his own needs, when he goes out to seek the love which he needs, no matter how we try to soften our judgments of him, he is self-centered. He is not loveable, even if he does deserve our compassion. He is concentrating on himself, and as long as he continues to concentrate on himself, his ability to love will always remain stunted and he will himself remain a perennial infant.

If, however, a person seeks not to receive love, but rather to give it, he will become loveable and he will most certainly be loved in the end. This is the immutable law under which we live: concern for ourself and convergence upon self can only isolate self and induce an even deeper and more torturous loneliness. It is a vicious and terrible cycle that closes in on us when loneliness, seeking to be relieved through the love of others, only increases.

The only way we can break this cycle formed by our lusting egos is *to stop being concerned with ourselves* and *to begin to be concerned with others.* This, of course, is not easy. To relocate the focus of one's mind from self to others can, in fact, mean a lifetime of effort and work. It is made more difficult because we must put others in the forefront, in place of ourselves. We must learn to respond to the needs of others without seeking the satisfaction of our own needs.

In his book, *Religion and Personality*, psychologist-priest Adrian van Kaam insists that if anyone seeks his own happiness and fulfillment, he will never find them; but adds that, if one does find his own happiness and fulfillment, it will be because he has forgotten himself to seek the happiness and fulfillment of those around him. The problem is that we are all clutching to our own life-rafts. We are tempted to fascination with our own self-fulfillment and everything we do is somehow designed to achieve our own safety and happiness. We can be selfish in very refined and subtle ways. Such preoccupation with self is an absolute obstacle to human happiness and fulfillment, because human happiness and fulfillment can be attained only through genuine love. Each of us must make a basic decision about how we intend to spend our lives. If we decide to spend our lives in the pursuit of our own happiness and fulfillment, we are destined to failure and desolation. If we decide to spend our lives seeking the fulfillment and happiness of others, and this is what is implied in love, we shall certainly attain our own happiness and fulfillment.

The person who wants only his own fulfillment, or who decides to love in order that he be fulfilled, will find that his love is in vain because the focus remains on himself. A person can grow only as much as his horizon allows, and the person who decides to love in order to be fulfilled and happy will be disappointed and will not grow because the horizon is still himself. Consequently, we cannot conceive of love in any way as a means of self-fulfillment, because if we do we will still be within the treacherous vicious circle, traveling always from our own needs through others and back into ourselves. We cannot ever use others as means. They must always be the end-object of love. We will attain maturity only in proportion to the shifting of the focus of our minds away from ourselves and our own needs and away from the self-centered desire to satisfy those needs.

Loving others can be truly accomplished only when the focus of our minds and the object of our desires is another, when all of our activity results from concern for another and not from concern for ourselves. We have said that if a person truly loves in this way, he will be loved and he should accept the love of others. However the delusion to be avoided at all costs is to love in order to receive this return. I must, as Christ suggests, lose my life before I can gain it. I must find out that the only real receiving is in giving. I have to lose my life and I cannot lose it if I always have it clearly before my own mind.

In other words, love means a concern for, acceptance of, and an interest in the others around me whom I am trying to love. It is a self-donation which may prove to be an altar of sacrifice. I can love others only to the extent they are truly the focus of my mind, heart, and life; and I can find myself only by forgetting myself. Love is indeed costly and demanding. Because of the inward pains that all of us bear, the scar tissues that are part of our human inheritance, because of the competition and example of a self-grasping world, it will be difficult for us to make the sacrifice of ourselves that is involved in loving. Loving always means at least this sacrifice, the orientation of my thoughts and desires towards others and the abandonment of my own self and self-interest. Needless to say, such abandonment always involves a high cost to self.

But if a life of love is difficult, it is not a bleak or unrewarding life. In fact, it is the only truly human and happy life for it is filled with concerns that are as deep as life, as wide as the whole world, and as far reaching as eternity. It is only when we have consented to love, and have agreed to forget ourselves, that we can find our fulfillment. It will come unperceived and mysterious like the Grace of God, but we will recognize it and it will be recognized in us. We will have made the Copernican revolution that relocates the focus of our minds and hearts on the good and fulfillment of others; and although this conversion has sought nothing for itself, it has received everything. The loveable person is, in the last analysis, the one who has made the consent to love.

So often we demand that others love us without being willing to make the sacrifice and abandonment of self that is necessary to become loveable. However, if anyone has mastered the delicate and profound paradox that love involves,

Most adults never grow up.

and has been willing to dedicate himself without reservation or demand for return to the needs and fulfillment of others, he will certainly be loved and fulfilled within himself.

But how can we love if we have never been loved? Between black and white there is always an area of gray. All of us have some capacity to love, some ability to move the focus of our minds out from ourselves to the needs, happiness, and fulfillment of others. To the extent that we do this, to the extent that we actualize this potential that is latent within us, we will be loved. Even if at the beginning we can love only a little, we shall be loved a little; and the love that we receive will empower us to grow more and more out of ourselves in the direction that love leads. This, then, is the challenge that lies before each of us: we must utilize whatever capacity, be it small or great, we have for love. To the extent that we are willing to make the effort and dedication that is involved, we will be nourished and strengthened by the love that we shall receive in return; but we must remember that, in making this self-donation, the focus of our minds must always be away from self and this precludes thinking of or asking for a return. When we ask that question: "What Have You Done For Me?" we have ceased to love.

Christ and Love

Christ our Lord left no doubt about the credential of the Christian. He said, "By this shall men know that you are my disciples, that you love one another . . . love one another as I have loved you . . . this is all I command you that you love one another." Saint John reminds us in his First Epistle that it is impossible to love God whom we do not see and not love those around us whom we do see.

All of these things we have read, and perhaps we pay them more lip service than life service. We know that Christ takes as done to himself what we do to others; he accepts as given to himself our concern and kindness for others. In the daily battle, however, when our own needs are so throbbing and painful, we forget.

The only attitude worthy of the Christian is that of Christ, who thought of others always, who gave himself until he had not another drop of blood to give. In his own words, "Greater love than this no man has than that he lay down his life for his friend." This is, of course, what love asks of us, that we lay down our lives for others. Only when we have consented to do this will we find ourselves, our own happiness and fulfillment, and only then will we be true Christians. If we fail to do this, perhaps there will be some justification in the questions that the agnostic philosopher, Nietzsche, once asked: "If Christians wish us to believe in their Redeemer, why don't they look a little more redeemed?" It was this same Nietzsche who coined the phrase, so sadly common in our own days: "God is dead."

Love of Christ in the Love of Christians

In the 1920's, the philosopher of American Communism was a Jew named Mike Gold. After communism fell into general disrepute in this country, Mike Gold became a man of oblivion. In this oblivion he wrote a book, *A Jew Without Knowing It.* In describing his childhood in New York City, he tells of his mother's instructions never to wander beyond four certain streets. She could not tell him that it was a Jewish ghetto. She could not tell him that he had the wrong kind of blood in his veins. Children do not understand prejudice. Prejudice is a poison that must gradually seep into a person's blood stream.

In his narration, Mike Gold tells of the day that curiosity lured him beyond the four streets, outside of his ghetto, and of how he was accosted by a group of older boys who asked him a puzzling question: "Hey, kid, are you a *kike*?" "I don't know." He had never heard the word before. The older boys came back with a paraphrase of their question. "Are you a Christ-killer?" Again, the small boy responded, "I don't know." He had never heard that word either. So the older boys asked him where he lived, and trained like most small boys to recite their address in the case of being lost, Mike Gold told them where he lived. "So you are a kike; you are a Christ-killer. Well you're in Christian territory and we are Christians. We're going to teach you to stay where you belong!" And so they beat the little boy, bloodied his face and tore his clothes and sent him home to the jeering litany: "We are Christians and you killed Christ! Stay where you belong! We are Christians, and you killed Christ . . .".

When he arrived home, Mike Gold was asked by his frightened mother: "What happened to you, Mike?" He could answer only: "I don't know." "Who did this to you, Mike?" Again he answered: "I don't know." And so the mother washed the blood from the face of her little boy and put him into fresh clothes and took him into her lap as she sat in a rocker, and tried to soothe him. Mike Gold recalled so much later in life that he raised his small battered lips to the ear of his mother and asked: "Mama, who is Christ?"

Mike Gold died in 1967. His last meals were taken at a Catholic Charity house in New York City, run by Dorothy Day. She once said of him: "Mike Gold eats every day at the table of Christ, but he will probably never accept him because of the day he first heard his name." And so he died.

For better or for worse Christ has taken us as his living symbols in this world. The world that is asking whether God is dead or not, the world that is asking who Christ is can find its answers only in the Christian. For better or for worse, we are Christ to the world.

Almost any other apologetic for the Christian faith can be memorized, rehearsed, and delivered without effect except the apologetic of love. Love, which of its essence seeks only the good of others and is willing to pay the high price of self-forgetfulness, is a product which is hard to imitate or counterfeit.

To love, one must have enormous motivation. In a grasping world, in a world which is gouging and clawing for the riches of this world, the Christian by his love must stand forth as a breathtaking exception. The true Christian must seek only the good, the fulfillment and the destiny of his fellow man. Love will always be his most eloquent argument and effective means. It is difficult. And yet the Lord Christ of the Gospels stands with us, and it becomes our Christian imperative: "By this shall men know that you are my disciples, that you love one another."